BECOMING BUKKI

BECOMING BUKKI

A Story Of Triumph Amidst Trials

BUKUNOLA POPOOLA

Bukunola

Contents

1 CHILDHOOD — 1
2 HIGHER EDUCATION — 8
3 ENTERING THE WORK FORCE — 16
4 MATRIMONY — 22
5 ENGLAND — 28
6 DIVORCE — 32
7 STARTING A NEW LIFE — 39

About The Author — 57

Copyright © 2023 by Bukunola Popoola

All rights reserved. No part of this book may be reproduced in any manner whatsoever without written permission except in the case of brief quotations embodied in critical articles and reviews.

First Printing, 2023

I

CHILDHOOD

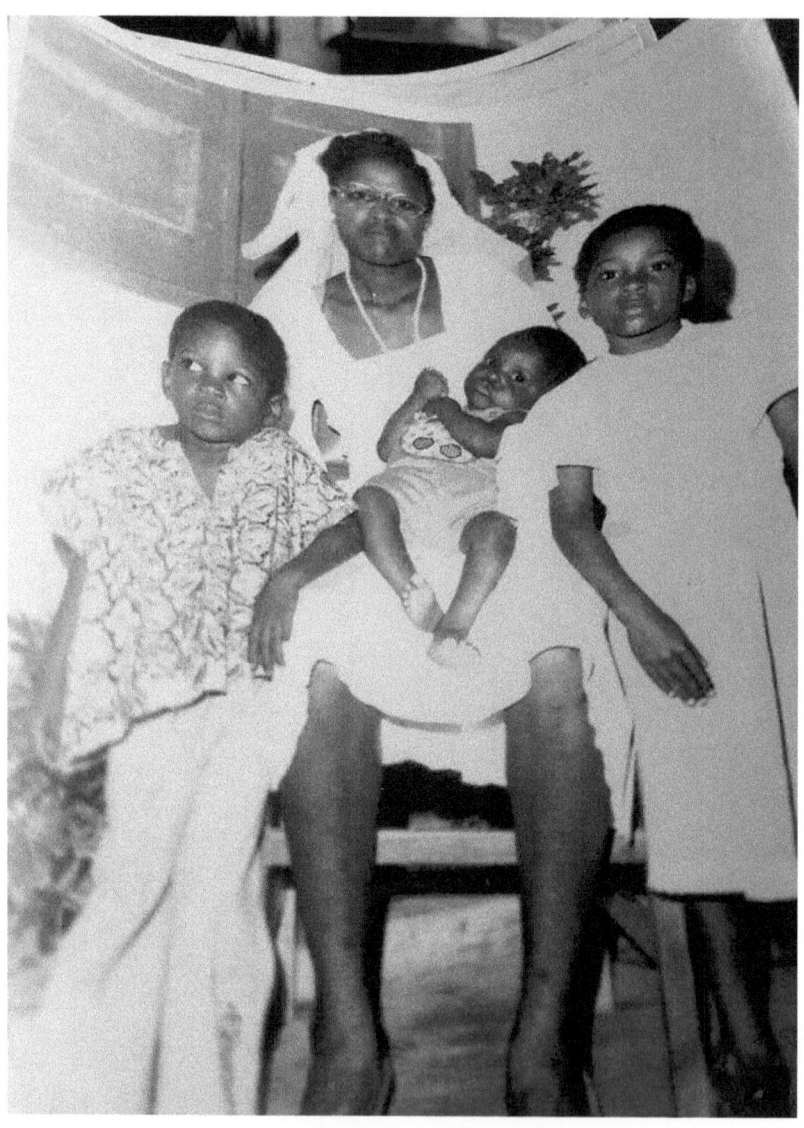

Me, my two immediate brothers and my aunty in Ibadan,
Nigeria, 1976/77
Bukki Popoola

I came to the UK as an adult; my childhood was in Africa – Nigeria, to be exact. I arrived on 11th March 1973; I don't know when I was born, but that is what they told me. I was born in Ibadan, Oyo state, in western Nigeria, and my childhood years panned between Ibadan and Lagos. I think I only visited the northern region – Kaduna – once in my lifetime. I have never been to the eastern part.

Mine was a pretty typical middle-class Nigerian family of the 1970s. It was a close setting, even with the cousins and other extended family members. I have many happy childhood memories. We went to the best schools. We mixed with good family members, family friends of a similar level – you know what I mean? I had my maternal grandparents at my beck and call! My grandfather was a land surveyor, which made him very rich in those days. My grandmother was a businesswoman; she had several shops selling fabrics. I went to a mixture of day and boarding schools, which was part of the whole experience and exposed me to how other people live and how to be independent because it helps you to develop into becoming the person you become.

I have five siblings, three boys and two girls, and then there is me, which makes six in total. My father is a mechanical engineer, and my mother is a housewife. He is retired now, and they live in Texas near one sibling. Three siblings now live in Canada, and one still lives in Nigeria. We are an international family. I am the only one living in England. I only found myself here because my ex-husband chose to live in England.

However, it was also a strict upbringing, and the rod was never spared, so to speak. There was pressure to be perfect, excel academically with expectations of entering a prestigious profession, and also be of exemplary behaviour. You grew up knowing you had to be perfect, which became even more prominent when Father became a pastor, which meant you had to be the standard for all the other children in the church. As I excelled at school, there wasn't too much concern for me at first. The main challenge was that, in my teenage years, I started to become a bit rebellious.

Mother was strict. When I say 'strict', she was always ready to beat the daylights out of you.

Father was approachable, though, always willing to sit with his children and talk. Usually, he took Mother's side to keep her happy and stay out of trouble. He came from poverty and learnt many life lessons, which he was always willing to share. You could not have a conversation with Mother; as far as she was concerned, if you were a child, you obeyed, as simple as that. I did not really have a relationship with her. If one of my younger siblings did something wrong, as the eldest, I would also get punished!

I took my father's style of parenting. Even if I wanted to, you're just not going to hit your child in England, you'll get into trouble. It's about understanding the child; is that (hitting) what they are going to respond to, or will it be detrimental to their development? I think smacking my child would make him close up, and I prefer we talk about issues. So far, talking has worked very well. But, I can't wait till he goes off to university because I can't deal with teenagers any more!

My favourite subjects were the sciences. I would not say I was the greatest fan of chemistry. I was more into mathematics, physics and biology. I would say biology was my favourite. I resonate more with biology because it is more of things you can see and understand and actually investigate and learn how they work. Ants have three sections in their body, I can see that, and it makes sense. But, if you give me an equation in physics and ask me to fathom that, I can do that, but it is not as exciting for me.

As I grew, I became more curious about the world beyond the parameters established by my upbringing. I just had to see what was out there, good or bad; I wanted to find out for myself. I wanted to go out and have boyfriends. Saying that, I must stress that I had my standards as well. I was not going to be the girl who sleeps with every guy. But I wanted the fun, to get away from that closed, controlled setting of home.

I quickly learnt to be two people. At home, I was what my parents expected me to be. I would sneak out of the house to hang out with friends and soon had a boyfriend (more of a pen pal, I suppose). One of my friends asked me if I had a boyfriend, and when I said that I did not have one, she introduced me to her brother. It wasn't sexual or anything; it was more just feeling grown up because I could now say I had a boyfriend.

When you have a boyfriend, you change without actually realising, you know. You pay more attention to your appearance, things like that. My parents soon noticed. So, they decided to whisk me off to a boarding school in Ondo State. I only became aware of this decision as we travelled to the neighbouring state.

My family, the Olusanya clan

With my father
Bukki Popoola

2

HIGHER EDUCATION

I found myself in a completely different school in a completely different state. I lost all contact with many good friends, as there was no chance to exchange addresses with them when I left Ibadan, and we did not have mobile phones in those days. I could only re-connect with some of these friends as an adult on social media.

My new school was in Akure, Ondo State. The principal was my guardian. She is still alive. She was a strict, no-nonsense kind of woman but warm and motherly. If you crossed boundaries, she would counsel you firmly and you would go off to think about what you had done. She was more like a mother to me than my own mother. I could talk to her as she understood young girls. Her children were grown up. I am still in touch with her and hold her in high esteem.

Returning home to Lagos during the mid-term break and some holidays didn't make sense to me, so I stayed at the principal's house. I enjoyed living there more than I did at my own home. My mother would nag until I did not want to do anything, and I still had to do as told. There was also the added stress of cleaning up after my younger siblings.

The principal taught me many things about life outside school, such as how to cook and dress farm animals; farms come with all sorts of wildlife, so we also had grasscutters (*Thyronomys Swinderianus*, the Giant Cane Rat). She taught me how to cook those. They are tasty!

'Bukki, did you know you are supposed to write your WAEC (West African Examination Council) exams?' The principal asked me one day.

My father did not go through the routine of attending secondary school, high school and university. He went through a technical college, and because he was brilliant, he obtained a scholarship to study engineering in Canada. My mother, as I mentioned earlier, was just a housewife. Neither of them would have known about the exams. If not for the principal, there wouldn't have been anyone to explain to me about registering for the exam.

The principal suggested I write trial exams in February and register for the one in August. Honestly, I did not take the exams seriously because I knew I would have another chance later in the year. However, fortunately (or unfortunately), those were the results I used to get into the University of Ilorin, Kwara State, to study Education and Mathematics. Fortunately, new rules got introduced the same year that said you could not sit for the WAEC exams twice in the same year. Unfortunately, the results were not that good. If not for the principal and one of my father's old schoolmates, a lecturer at the university, I wouldn't have known how to secure my admission to the university.

Uni life is another ballgame. Initially, I was a naive girl. My expectations were high. My father had left paid employment and started his own business. The company wasn't giving anything for those last few years, so the family was floating. I expected to start uni with a totally new wardrobe – the teenage mindset. Well, I didn't get that. I was so disappointed. How was I supposed to go to uni without the things I saw my peers getting?

My grandmother was poorly, so she was staying with us in Lagos. When she saw me crying, declaring that I wasn't going to uni without new, trendy clothes, she asked me what exactly I needed. I told her. 'Well, I have some wrappers,' she said, 'Take them with you; you can make whatever you want out of them.' Can you imagine?

The allowance my father could afford to give me was only enough for the long trip from Lagos across four or five states to Ilorin. You could say my life at university was this low-level lifestyle. I wasn't part of the trendy, happening crowd because I did not have the fashionable things that they had. So, I just kept my head down and focused on my studies. I made some friends local to Ilorin, and they took me to thrift shops, where I could get a few items.

It was not a case of me desperately wanting to fit in and feeling frustrated. I was only trying to see what was out there in the world that I had been closed off from by my upbringing. I just wanted to be like the other girls. Right from a young age, I realised the kind of person I wanted to be and worked towards that goal. I won't say I am what I want to be right now. Obviously, life has happened, and it has derailed the journey a little bit here and there, but I have no regrets about being who I am today.

I had my fair share of boyfriends and relationships, too. At that age, you don't have a clue. You do whatever you want to do. It's OK; everybody is doing it. So, I had male friends, and I had female friends. Obviously, I stayed within my cadre. I wasn't wayward or promiscuous or anything like that. I just wanted to see what was out there and understand why wasn't allowed there. I can count the number of men I have dated on my fngers.

There were up to two and a half years of strike action by university lecturers, and we could not attend classes. As a result, it took six years for me to finish my degree. So, during the strike, I was just at home. I was in a relationship then, so I spent most of my time with my guy. I would sneak in there and sneak out, which was typical.

I dated a guy from a high-class Muslim family in my first year. We spent time together, and I even met the family in their home. The father was a doctor, and my boyfriend was studying medicine, but I was thinking, 'He's a nice guy, but he's a Muslim, and I am a Christian. What is going to be the balance of this? Is there a future? Better to get out now before it's too late.'

I never told my own family I was dating a Muslim. I had an idea of what the reaction would be. So, I left him and met another guy who was also a Muslim but not very strict. I don't know what it was with me and Muslim guys! I guess I am a free-natured person. If I liked a guy, I liked them. I would later ask myself if there was a future in the relationship. I did not see the background, rich, poor, so long as you are nice. I just wanted the person and not what was around the person.

We dated for a while with this second guy. Then, at some point, I found out that he cheated on me with a friend and that he had cheated on his previous girlfriend with me, all on the same campus. So, we broke up. I started another relationship and soon discovered I was pregnant.

It was a school holiday, and I did not know what to do. I took myself to the family doctor, and he confirmed that I was pregnant. 'Why don't you keep the baby?' he asked when I said I wanted to get rid of it.

'One, because I am a student,' I said. 'And, two, because my parents will kill me.'

Fortunately for me, he not only took it out, but he never informed my parents. Abortion is illegal in Nigeria, by the way.

I told the guy. He did not know what to do; we were both students in Africa in the late '80s/early '90s. In those days, there was not much information about condoms or contraceptives. It was taboo to say you were having sex. He was caring, to be fair, and supportive of my decision to terminate the pregnancy. We have remained friends.

In my estate, there were ten blocks of flats each; in another building, there was a girl my age, and we became friends. During the lecturer's strike, we hung out together often. We decided to look for jobs. One of our neighbours owned a publishing company. So we approached him. He invited us to his office; when we went, he said he had work to do and asked me to return.

I did not have the knowledge I now have about these things. He was leading me on about the job. Eventually, he sexually assaulted me. I didn't report him because I didn't know how. The knowledge I have these days, I did not have it back then. And society did not have the understanding that it has now. Everything would just be quiet. I didn't know who to tell.

The experience has made me want to have those 'difficult' discussions with my son about sexual health, condoms and sexuality. I have told him he should come to me if anything happens. I never had such conversations with my parents.

When I returned to uni, I discovered I was pregnant again. I tried to contact the publisher, but he blocked me. After three months, I had to tell one of my friends. She took me to this doctor and paid for the abortion. The doctor had a talk with me about safe sex. I resolved to learn my body, so I would know the safe periods to have sex (remember, condoms were unavailable). Some people took a pill in the morning after unprotected sex, but I was anxious about what it would do to my body. When I got married and wasn't getting pregnant, I was scared that the pill or the abortions had damaged my body for life, but that was not the case.

My next relationship ran for several years. We were going to get married. He had finished uni and was working. He was my friend's brother, the same friend I had gone to look for a job with. We had a good time, but he did not really know what he wanted. He did not discard me as such but stuck with me while he studied other women. You know this African mentality of us not being brought up with a proper understanding of your needs and wants and how things should be? I think Africa did a lot of that with that generation of mine. My parents never had open and honest conversations with their children.

We didn't get married, but we remained in contact. One day, a friend of his told me, 'Ask him what he wants because someone else is coming!'

I asked him, and he admitted that he didn't know how it happened, but there was this girl was saying she was pregnant by him. He said he did not want her and wasn't even sure the pregnancy was his. I guess the girl was persuasive – before you knew it, they were married.

We remained friends. When he was struggling and needed someone to turn to, it was Bukki. When he needed advice, it was Bukki. He came to pick me up at the airport when I last visited Nigeria, but I did not stay at his house. His wife is deceased now, leaving him with four children. She died of cancer, and he lost everything to pay for the treatment, which had to be in Dubai. He battles with depression. If he wants to talk, I listen, but that is all there is to the relationship now. I said, 'You didn't want me when you were doing OK. I don't want you now.' Why should I be the one to pick up the pieces? I would rather be by myself.

So, over the years, when we got talking, he mentioned that the only reason he was sceptical about being with me was my mother. He said he knew what she could be like and did not want a mother-in-law like that, which was a fair point; my mum can be a little bit too much. She doesn't see herself as such, but now, with my understanding of mental health, I wonder if she is bipolar or has a personality disorder which went undiagnosed.

My mother and I have had no contact since I refused to feed their excesses when I completed my degree. My parents wanted me to come over to the States to look after them in their old age, and leave the life I was making here in the UK. 'There are some things you do not say to people,' I told my father, 'You don't have to tell me I need to come and look after you because I know what I have to do. That is a bit too much.'

My mother must have overheard this conversation and has not spoken to me since.

As a student nurse, University of Northampton
Bukki Popoola

3

ENTERING THE WORK FORCE

In Nigeria, we had a National Youth Service where graduates went somewhere for one year. Many people have connections in Nigeria. You must know somebody who knows somebody for you to get something. So, if you are not in the right circles, it can set you back quite a lot. For me, I found myself in the middle. I couldn't say we were low, low, but we were not high up. One of my father's pastor friends was a director at a Community Bank in Lagos. He used this connection to ensure I stayed with the bank after my National Service.

I worked with the community bank for a while. It wasn't bad; I had money and lived on and off at home.

At one point, I got a self-contained apartment in a mansion owned by a dodgy older woman. It was a beautiful house in the Maryland area, an affluent part of Lagos. But the owner was weird. She was doing all sorts of things in her house that I could not understand; I think she was into witchcraft or sorcery because she had a separate space near my apartment. She brought in people in the middle of the night. There were people you saw around the house for about a week, and then you never saw them again. She changed housemaids often, and I would ask, 'What happened to that one?' And she would be like, 'Oh, she's a bad girl, that one – she's gone. She was a bad girl.'

I suspect she also forced her maids to engage in bestiality with her. And she was always trying to invite me to her events. Although I was curious, I never went! I tried to peep through the window, but I could never tell what exactly she was doing. All I knew was something wasn't right, and I wasn't safe there. I stayed at this strange house for about five months.

I mentioned this situation to one of the big aunties I worked with. 'Why don't you move in with me?' she said. 'I have three bedrooms, and my husband is always away, staying with one of his girlfriends.'

I stayed with her for a long time, and she was pleasant. I could have stayed home, but my parents' house was far from work.

I believe in doing your job to the best of your ability because I know that is what pays you. Even up to now, I don't joke with my job. I worked well at the New Life Community Bank, everyone liked me, and I knew one of the directors, so I was safe.

One day, I saw this guy come into the bank. I supervised the cashiers and sat by myself. To my surprise, he asked to see me; this was the first time I saw him, but he said he knew me. He ended up being my ex-husband.

He said he attended my church the previous week and first saw me. He had made enquiries and found out where I worked. But that was all fibs. I later discovered that one of our family friends was his aunt, who set us up without my knowledge. She had told him where he could find me.

We were already dating when I discovered he was related to this family friend. I suspect my parents also knew about this setup but never said a thing. I knew they were thinking, 'She's finished uni; she's got a job – it is time to get married.' You know these expectations. So, they set me up for this failure.

He was OK, so we started dating. I mean, he wasn't bad looking. He wasn't rich, but that wasn't a bother to me, as I had money and was not looking to rely on him for anything. I wasn't with anyone, which is probably why they all felt they had to step in and set me up with this guy.

And then, as we went along, I started doubting marrying this guy. I am looking at everything about him and thinking, 'Is this what I want?'

When I expressed these doubts to my parents, they would shut me up, saying, 'There is nothing wrong with him; he is great – it's you who is not being serious here.'

I was in my late twenties, but you know how it is with African families. Being twenty-eight meant that, in their eyes, I was old, and they would not see me blow what they saw as probably my last chance to get married. It's an African thing – that African thing screws us all, especially females. For males, they do not care, but if you are a female, then you need to start making babies.

I started noticing that he told little lies. 'Oh, but he lies!' I said, but my family wouldn't hear any of it. And everyone around me was just like, 'All men lie.'

It turned out that he was just a gold digger. He came from a not-so-good background and had seen a chance with my family. They didn't see any of this, I did, and I just went along with it. Now, I can challenge anyone because, in England, you have the confidence to do that. As long as you are right in what you are saying and know precisely what you are doing, no one will say no to you. But, in Africa, you can't even speak your mind.

I had doubts, and even at the last minute, I was ready to back out of the relationship, but my auntie joined in and said to me, 'You know what, there are challenges everywhere. Maybe he's not as bad as you are making him out to be.'

And that is how I got into this marriage after six months of dating.

Mother and son selfie.
Bukki Popoola

BECOMING BUKKI

4

MATRIMONY

We had a lavish wedding sponsored by my parents. In Nigeria, it is normal for the bride's family to do this and make it a grand occasion. Looking back, I think my husband saw the wedding as his way of telling the world that he had arrived. The wedding was for them – my husband and my parents – and not for me. I remember thinking that this was only right. In Africa, you cannot challenge your parents. They tell you what to do and how to do it, and that's it.

It wasn't long before my husband's true colours began to show. He started seeing other women and did not even try to hide the affairs. You can't even think of backing out because; how dare you even think of walking out of your marriage? For my parents, how could a pastor's daughter walk out of a union? It was easier for me to leave the betrothal when I was in England because I knew my rights and could stand up for myself.

The worst part of the marriage was his family. Every single one of Mum's side of the polygamous family was horrible; they did not like me. I look back now and think that the problem was that our backgrounds were different. I come from one where you wake up and say 'morning' to each other as a family. My in-laws were traditional. The youngest family member expected you to kneel before him and say, 'Good morning; what can I do for you? What would you like to eat?'

I was not used to that. I did not even know anyone who did that! Perhaps it would have been easier if my husband had sat me down and explained that this was how they did things in his family, but he was never interested in helping to improve relations between his family and me. All he was after was improving himself by marrying me, which he did.

We got an apartment, but one of my husband's aunts, a lecturer at a university, suggested we have our honeymoon there. In that one week we were there, I noticed that my husband preferred to spend more time with his relatives than with me. He would sit with his relatives for hours while I felt unwelcome.

My father-in-law did not attend the wedding because he was bedridden. He passed away after the wedding. There were eight children, three before my mother-in-law married my husband's dad. There were three boys and five girls. He had never mentioned this, and I only found out after we married about the family dynamics and exactly how many siblings he had. Throughout our dating, he had given the impression that his family was similar to mine. If my parents inquired, that family friend, who was my husband's aunt, would have reassured them that everything was OK.

At the funeral, I got called by the family. They made this massive circle around me.

'Your father-in-law is dead now,' they told me, 'And your mother-in-law is going to be living with you.'

Where is my husband? He has gone off to hide because he has already been spoken to and doesn't know how to face me with this decision of his family's! If he had been in my shoes at that point, I would have defended him; I would have said to them, 'No, you can't do this to her. Can you talk to me instead?'

He did not do any of that. He would just hide somewhere and leave them to harass me.

Our apartment had a lounge area, a bedroom, a kitchenette, a shower and a toilet. It was a bachelor pad. When we returned from the honeymoon, we found that the mother, the mother's sister and his cousin had settled in. I was like, 'What are all these people doing here?'

'Don't worry, don't worry, I am going to sort it out,' he said. Did he ever sort it out?

My husband was working for a plastics company. He never came clean about what he did there and just said he was one of the supervisors or managers. I think he was just a junior officer.

Hell was better than my life in that flat! As if having the three of them was not bad enough, his older siblings from my mother-in-law's previous marriage were daily visitors from morning till night. And they expected me not to go to work but wait on them hand and foot. It wasn't one month into the marriage before we started having issues. But he did not care; he wasn't bothered. Then the beatings began. His mother encouraged him, saying, 'She is not listening; you must teach her a lesson.'

She would report me to him in my presence.

I spoke to my parents, told them what I was facing, and said I could not cope. They sympathised with me, but because of the stigma around divorce, they wouldn't let me leave the marriage. They decided to find us another apartment. Through a member of their church, they got us a three-bedroomed apartment. My brother in Texas spoke to his manager at the bank where he worked and sealed my husband a job.

It wasn't long before his mother moved into our new apartment!

This time, I didn't know beforehand that she was coming. 'Oh, she is still bereaved and needs looking after,' he said.

By who?

The beatings continued and his siblings from his mum encouraged him. I became an outcast in my own house. My husband began to ignore me when I greeted him as he returned from work. The mother would rush before me to open the door for him, and they would head straight to her bedroom. That would be the last I saw of them. The mother would say, 'Oh, she starved me all day; she hasn't given me food.'

Yet whenever I asked her what she wanted to eat, she would say she was OK. One day, he went into the kitchen, saying he would make her some food himself. I told him, 'You know, you are stupid. If your mother had said she was starving, the onus is on you to come to me and ask me to make her some food. You don't go into the kitchen; you did not even buy anything in this kitchen.'

My mother-in-law had no boundaries at all. She would wash my husband's underwear, saying I wasn't capable.

They would say, 'She's barren!' because I wasn't pregnant yet.

But how could I get pregnant when I wasn't intimate with my husband?

The mother spent three years with us. She has never expressed shame or remorse for her actions. Eventually, my mother confronted my mother-in-law and said, 'If you don't leave this house, I am moving in too!'

When my parents left for the United States, they left us their five-bedroom house. My in-laws moved and still came around and stayed for long periods, but I had begun to put my foot down. Before my parents left, my mother called my husband and me, having found out about the UK's HSMV (Highly Skilled Migrant Visa), and said, 'As long as you keep living with your in-laws, the problems will continue. You need to relocate.'

I also found out I was pregnant. I can tell you precisely the day I got pregnant because I had started to ensure I had sex when ovulating. That day, he was doing every single thing to frustrate me.

'Are you coming in?'

He said. 'I told you I will come when I am ready.'

'I told you I need to have sex today; can you please come?' 'Well, I don't have time for you today.'

He had it in his head that I was barren, so he did not see the point in sleeping with me.

'OK,' he said as he entered the bedroom, 'Take off your clothes, then!'

I took my clothes and lay there, and he was out. It was disgusting, but I told myself to stay calm. I felt pity for myself. I asked myself what had happened for me to become like this.

Fortunately, I got pregnant. When I went to the doctor for a pregnancy test, the nurse said, 'You have been coming here for a long time. If you are pregnant, you are pregnant, stop having doubt, go home and keep praying.'

In Africa, everything is prayer. I told my husband. He did not believe I was pregnant at first.

'How many times have you said you were pregnant?' he said.

It was a good thing he did not believe me. Otherwise, the news would have been all over the place.

Three months into the pregnancy, I started bleeding. I was rushed to the hospital, put on bed rest for a week and monitored.

'Please, this is a precious baby, and you need to take care of it,' the doctor told me, 'Whatever he says to you, don't think about it or take it to heart. Just focus on you and the baby.'

When the time came, the baby wasn't coming out or even turning into position. I walked; I pounded with a mortar and pestle, anything to make the baby come. I had to have a caesarean section. My child had jaundice, and I lost blood.

My in-laws were bitter that I did not let my mother-in-law stay with us at the new house. They did not contribute a single kobo towards the hospital bill totalling a hundred thousand naira. My husband was delighted he had a son. When he told his mother the news, she said, 'I will come and see them when I can.'

My husband's older sister came to the hospital on the fifth day. She did not even hold my child. She said something I will never forget, 'Mama (the mother-in-law) says she will come to see your baby, but she won't come now because there is no one to look after the chickens.'

She came on the seventh day. My mum forced the baby into her hands, saying, 'Ah, ah, Mama, are you not going to carry the baby? Take the baby, take the baby.'

She was not going to touch him or anything. I was looking at my mother and thinking, 'Why are you forcing her to carry the child if she doesn't want to?'

My mum was winking at me as if to say, 'No, we don't do things like that. Just leave them.'

It took nearly five years in that marriage before I finally got pregnant – five years of being called barren and useless to my face.

By that time, my mother-in-law had left our house. My husband was not paying the rent he had agreed to; he contributed nothing towards the household expenses. I was looking after the baby, the house, everything. He was still nasty to me. Eventually, my mum said, 'You guys need to leave this country; otherwise, you will never have a life.'

She got the application forms for the HSMV from the agent, a church member. She told me, 'Bukki, with how your husband behaves, you should be the principal in this application. You have everything it requires.'

But I said, 'He's the husband, let him do it. I don't want to go through the hassle of the application process.'

5

ENGLAND

We landed at London's Heathrow Airport and went straight to Northampton, where we had our only contact in the country; my husband's brother's ex-girlfriend. She got us a room at a lovely three-storey townhouse a stone's throw from where she lived. The rooms had no heating, it was August when we came to Britain, and it was freezing! We had to boil water in a kettle to wash. My son was only two years, one-month-old.

I was ready to do any job. Yes, I had a university education, but I understood we needed to start somewhere in this country. We had to pick anything until we had learnt the system here; this is what everyone else was doing. I already knew the person I was with, that wasn't going to be doing anything for me. So, I was going through all the adverts and applying for everything; cleaning, whatever. Our landlady knew someone with an agency who would offer us some jobs. I was sending applications every week, and I was getting jobs. I didn't care if it was two pounds or four pounds or whatever pounds, so long as something was coming in.

What was my husband applying for? All the management roles he could find! After all, we had come to this country under the HSMV, so he certainly wasn't going to take whatever job that was available if it wasn't in the category of "highly-skilled. The worst part was that he wasn't looking after the child while I worked. He would tell me to go and give my child to a childminder. I would have to pay the childminder. He wouldn't buy anything in the home. Even right before I left him, he would not do anything except pay the rent. I tried to discuss this, but he would push me away.

We moved to a house where we had three rooms. However, we were still using one room, as he sublet the others to his two friends. He also had a job as a security guard. I was doing whatever I could find because I had a young child to look after. Unfortunately, my child wasn't speaking. So he felt, 'Oh, this child is no good,' and did not want to have anything to do with him.

When my child would come to him, he would say, 'Go, go, go to your mother!' and send him away.

He minded other people's children in the community. On his days off, he would phone his friend and offer to look after his child, but he did not want his own around.

My child did not speak until he was six. Specialists say this was due to trauma. One day, he just started talking. He did not even have to learn words; he had known them all this time. He told me everything his father had been doing to him.

My husband expected me to cook, wait on his friends and clean up after them since I was the only woman in the house. I essentially had three husbands, yet I still needed to pay someone to mind the child when I went to work. How he spoke to me in front of them made me feel worthless. I started to keep myself out of the room if his friends were present. My husband's friends saw the way he treated me, but they never confronted him about it. They would express their sympathy to me and say they thought what he did was wrong, but they would never say it to him. I put up with this because I thought, at some point, he would ask himself if this was how things should be and change.

My in-laws were still very much in the picture. I overheard conversations on the landline extension downstairs, urging him to split up with me. They were sore about me not letting his mother remain in my parents' house when we left Nigeria for England. He could not tell them I had bought and paid for everything in our home – he would have nothing if we separated. They never spoke to me on the phone.

I started to feel unsafe when my husband began to communicate with a herbalist in Nigeria. What if he poisoned me? I called my parents in America and told them I could not live like this anymore. My father said, 'Marriage should be enjoyed, not endured. If you think it is time to go, make your decision and whatever decision you make, we'll support you.'

I now had a regular job at a care home. I went and found myself a house. I redirected my mail to that house. I had planned to leave peacefully. I had arranged for a van to come when he would be at work. I was going to leave a note.

Unfortunately, Royal Mail sent a copy of the redirection notice to the old address.

First month in the UK, August 2007
Bukki Popoola

6

DIVORCE

My husband waited for me when I came home from a night shift. I had passed by the childminder's and taken my son to school.

'You think you are clever!' my husband said as soon as I had shut the door behind me.

I had already been to the police station, explained my situation and the plan to leave the next day. They had offered to come with me, but I had refused, knowing that their presence would only aggravate things. So, they gave me a number to call if I needed support.

Usually, I did not exchange words with him. But this time, when he started threatening me with violence, I said, 'What's the worst that could happen? Bring it on!'

So, I gave him a piece of my mind. He responded, 'I will beat the living daylights out of you! I will kill you.'

'Do it!' I said. 'And that is the last thing you will do.' He was shocked. 'Am I the one you are talking to?' He went up the stairs and down again.

'Yes!' I said. 'Do your worst! All these years, I am tired now! I am not doing this anymore. To be clear, I am separating myself from you to give you time to reflect and think if you still want this.'

He said, 'You'll see!'

As I walked past, he grabbed my neck. I went ballistic and gave it back to him. He ran out of the house as I looked for something to hit him with. I picked up the phone and started calling the police. I think he heard me call them.

When he came back, bouncing in, the police were with me. He approached me, and the police held him back. 'This is my house,' he said. 'At this point, you are being violent, and this woman is not safe with you,' the police said.

They asked me if I wanted to remain in the house, which meant he would have to leave.

I felt that if I stayed, there would be more problems, and he would tell people in Africa, 'She sent me packing from my own house.'

So the police took my husband away and said they would release him after I had finished packing and left the property. He couldn't believe what was happening.

My husband put his version of what happened on the community rumour mill. 'She left me. She took everything; she took my things!'

Even people who knew me accepted his version. Everyone was talking about it. 'She's found another man.'

'She's a woman; she should have been patient with him.'

Even the church said the same thing. 'I decide what is good for my life and what isn't,' I responded. 'If any of you think what I had was good, put yourself in that situation!'

I got exiled by the whole community – I could tell they were gossiping about me when I walked the streets. That did not deter me, but the truth is, I was struggling. For one, I was still my husband's dependent on his visa. I tried to have a civil discussion, but he would not accept it. I soon discovered that his family had already found a wife for him in Nigeria.

I went on anti-depressants. I could not sleep, worrying about the visa. But I kept pushing because I knew that was my only option. I don't know what he told them at the Home Office, but he only applied for himself when the time came to renew.

I made application after application and got the lawyers involved, but I got refusal after refusal. The Home Office's position was that my son and I depended upon the principal applicant, so we could not apply separately. My husband refused to discuss the issue with me. So, between 2012 and 2017, my son and I lived illegally in this country. Going back to Nigeria was not an option. I had given up my job to come here, and nearly all my family lived abroad now.

I was honest with my employers about my immigration status. They allowed me to continue working. I kept them up to date on the application process. Then, in 2015, my right to appeal was exhausted. I approached my employers and told them I did not want to get them into trouble with the Home Office, so I would stop working for them. They were confused; I don't think anyone has ever voluntarily stopped working for them because of immigration problems before! 'We appreciate your integrity,' the HR Director said. 'When do you think you will get sorted?'

I told them I did not know. They kept me for a month.

What turned the tide in my favour was my husband taking me to court for custody of our child. He acted pompous throughout the proceedings because he was taking me to court. I was feeling low; I had many other things to worry about. I did not have papers; I had to pay for everything and was in debt and living off payday loans. And he's walking the streets not thinking about giving his child even £5!

I told the judge, 'I never stopped him from seeing the child. He chose not to see him. My child had developmental challenges. He doesn't know him; how can he be expected to look after our child?'

The judge was a woman. She must have seen a lot in her career because she could immediately see what was happening. She recommended mediation for us and adjourned the case for two weeks.

He was angry. He had thought the court would hand over our child to him. What plans did he have for the boy? He was going to send him to Nigeria to spite me! All because I had dented his ego by walking out of the marriage. He stormed out of the court and did not even speak to the boy.

My former husband lives in Northampton, less than five minutes from us.

In the first week of the mediation, we agreed on contact and had to discuss support in the second week, but then he said he was no longer interested in mediation. The authorities could not force him to attend. I got advice to go to Child Maintenance. As immigrants, having never received child benefits, we were not in the system. It took years, but eventually, we got the go-ahead to obtain child maintenance.

Recently, my son and I ran into him in Aldi. He had a little child because he remarried. He said to me, 'How is my son?'

He hadn't recognised his son, who had just walked past him. I called our son back. 'Oh, is this you? Oh, you're wearing dreadlocks now.'

There was nothing between them at all, no connection.

England: Left, during the years of domestic abuse and violence. Right, when I started getting my life back

Early days after the best decision of my life, leaving my abusive husband. A hard decision, but the best decision ever
Bukki Popoola

7

STARTING A NEW LIFE

I got my Limited Leave To Remain and enrolled for my nursing degree. Can you believe that the woman came out of the office where she had gone to check my details and said to me right there before my friends, 'We can't enrol you because Home Office has refused your papers.'

I had to pay international student fees, £15,500, which included a deposit of £5,000.

'Can I pay just £2,000 for now?' I asked.

I did not even have £200; they would not accept anything less than £5,000. I said I would get back to them and had to leave the queue.

My world crashed. I do not know how I got home. I drove, but my head was banging, with one of those headaches where your vision goes. When I got home, I had some food and a rest and got into action. Scrolling down my contacts list on my phone, I called everyone and told them I needed money urgently. They all gave stories and excuses until I reached a man with a shop specialising in African groceries. We had not known each other for that long, I think I had only bought things from him about once or twice, but sometimes your angels are not the people you have known. They are people that God will send your way.

Ayo as an Army cadet
Bukki Popoola

'How much do you need?' he asked. 'Ten thousand pounds,' I said. 'I don't have, but I know somebody that can loan you the money,' he said. 'However, he will charge you some interest. I will be your guarantor because he doesn't want people to know that this is what he does.'

I agreed.

A few minutes later, I got a call, 'He's happy to lend you the money at 20% interest over a year.'

He invited me to the shop the next day to do the paperwork. And that is how I got the money to start uni. I could see myself paying this loan back in three years.

They were surprised to see me at uni. 'You can't enrol; you haven't paid.'

'I have – can you check your system.' My heart was beating fast. What if they checked and it said I hadn't?

'Oh, the system is down.'

'That's not my problem,' I said. 'I've paid. I need to be in class.'

Imagine my friends' surprise when I walked in and sat at the back.

It wasn't easy. Fortunately, my son was a bit grown by then. We did not have much time together. I was coming when he was going and going when he was coming. But I was always on the phone or sending text messages, don't get into trouble, don't do this, don't do that, be good. Mum will be home at this time.

He had to look after himself for most of his growing years. I look at him now and do not think we have done terribly. Many children in that situation wouldn't have come out as good as him. My son had no father figure except his uncle, my ex- husband's older brother. My former brother-in-law disagrees with what his younger brother did. My ex does not speak to his brother because of me.

After all that hard work, my dissertation failed. I resubmitted and failed again, this time by two marks. In my head, I thought, 'How do I get around this now?'

I had a job waiting for me – an allocated ward and uniform ordered. I had to tell them I had failed and could not start. I was in bed for almost a week, crying, not knowing what to do. Then, four days into my 'depression period,' I told myself I needed to get up and sort myself out. So, I repeated a module. Lucky for me, Covid happened, so we were doing remote learning, and no one saw that I was repeating classes! I noticed my supervisor was being funny again, so I requested a meeting.

'If I am doing anything wrong, please can you let me know? My previous supervisor never said anything – I just got a fail with no warning. If you are unhappy with my work, I would like you to correct me.'

'Oh, if I am unhappy with your work, I will say,' she said.

After that, she wouldn't respond to my emails. No comments on my work. I was like, This is going the same way again. So I emailed the Head of Module: I am just wondering if my supervisor is OK because I have been sending her emails and getting no reply. Is she off sick or anything?

That was the day I got a response from her. She wasn't happy and said I could ask the Head of Module to give me another supervisor if I did not want to work with her.

'I want to work with you,' I said. 'I wasn't sure if you wanted to work with me because I never hear from you.' Since that day, we communicated well.

I passed with a First-Class Honours degree. I was proud of myself. If I could achieve this as a single mother with no benefits and lots of debt, I had a right to be proud. A job awaited me, and I started as a nurse.

Life has taught me many things: Have confidence in yourself. Be true to yourself. You need to be able to face it all. For me, I'm a whole person. I don't care what the world says. Anything I choose to do, if I am convinced, then I am going to go for it.

Socially, I am more integrated. I have friends from Nigeria and other African nations, alongside Polish, Caribbean, and English. I do not discriminate. If you are happy to be my friend, I am pleased to be yours.

I am a shy person. I don't look people in the eye when I talk to them. People who don't know me say I am rude, proud or cocky. But this is my way of keeping myself in check, as I can get taken advantage of. If you are doing anything wrong and need telling off, I will do so. Some might call that rude, but I am just being honest.

I have benefited so much from my employer, a specialist hospital, which I always think, 'How do I give back? What can I do to make things better?'

So I am always putting myself forward for self-development programmes. I am so busy that I don't even remember that I do not have a boyfriend!

I know that my son is intelligent. I see a lot of me in him. Maybe he grew into that because he was always around me. He is planning to go to university. He got a job and said he is saving because he wants his bachelor pad to be nice! I tell him that if he wants something, he must work for it.

He opened an account you can't withdraw from until a set time passes. He gets up at 3 a.m. and cycles one-and-a-half hours to work a shift that starts at 6. I was discouraging him at first. But I like his attitude because he will look after his family. His father would stay at home and take all of my money. I feel I have shifted that. In a way, growing up without his Dad around has broken a pattern of behaviour that he would have probably picked up. Father and son are nothing alike.

I don't have much of a social life. I don't go to Nigerian parties much. I find the pressure to present a particular image to the community hard to deal with. My life primarily revolves around work, including few social activities, and my cosy space called home – my happy place.

I haven't done too terribly, considering where I have been and what I have gone through. Timescales are irrelevant. I am looking to the next 20 years of my life, and I know they will be better.

THE END

Receiving my BSc in Nursing (Mental Health) at Northampton University
Bukki Popoola

Always find a reason to laugh and live
Bukki Popoola

My 45th Birthday, celebration of a new era
Bukki Popoola

Nothing phases me. I am unstoppable
Bukki Popoola

Confident African beauty
Bukki Popoola

Ayomide stayed on track despite all the challenges along the way
Bukki Popoola

I won't change you for the world.....my one and only
Bukki Popoola

My child, the ace
Bukki Popoola

Ayomi, my joy, my pride, my son, my one and only
Bukki Popoola

100%
THANKFUL

100% thankful for the insight and determination to make the choice to be a better me: Divorce is not 'DELETE'
Bukki Popoola

I won't change you for the world ... my one and only

My child, the ace

Ayomi, my joy, my pride, my son, my one and only

100% thankful for the insight and determination to make the choice to be a better me. Divorce is not 'DELETE'

Bukunola "Bukki" Popoola (nee Fasanya) was born on the 11th of March 1973 in Ibadan, Oyo state, Nigeria, the first child in a family of six. She attended Children's Home School, Molete, Ibadan, Our Lady of Apostles Secondary School, Odo-Ona, Ibadan and continued her secondary education at Fiwasaye Girl's Grammar School, Akure, Ondo State. She studied Education/Mathematics at University of Ilorin, Kwara State, after which she worked at New Life Community Bank, Agidingbi, Lagos before relocating with her ex-husband and son to the United Kingdom.

Bukki is now a registered Mental Health Nurse and works as a Senior Staff Nurse in Northampton.
She lives in Northampton with her son.

Milton Keynes UK
Ingram Content Group UK Ltd.
UKHW011015020923
427894UK00004B/192